An Overview of

Sixteen Trends

Their Profound Impact on Our Future

Implications for Students, Education, Communities, and the Whole of Society

By Gary Marx

Educational Research Service
1001 North Fairfax Street, Suite 500, Alexandria, VA 22314
Tel: 703-243-2100 or 800-791-9308
Fax: 703-243-1985 or 800-791-9309
Email: ers@ers.org • Web site: www.ers.org

Educational Research Service is the nonprofit organization serving the research and information needs of the nation's K-12 education leaders and the public. Founded by the national school management associations, ERS provides quality, objective research and information that enable local school district administrators to make the most effective school decisions, both in terms of day-to-day operations and long-range planning.

ERS e-Knowledge Portal:
http://portal.ers.org

ERS Founding Organizations:
American Association of School Administrators
American Association of School Personnel Administrators
Association of School Business Officials International
National Association of Elementary School Principals
National Association of Secondary School Principals
National School Public Relations Association

Ordering information: Additional copies of *An Overview of Sixteen Trends . . . Their Profound Impact on Our Future* may be purchased at the base price of $14 each (ERS School District Subscriber price: $7; ERS Individual Subscriber price: $10.50). Quantity discounts available. Stock No. 0633. ISBN 1-931762-52-X.

Order from: Educational Research Service, 1001 North Fairfax Street, Suite 500, Alexandria, VA 22314. Telephone: 800-791-9308. Fax: 800-791-9309. Email: ers@ers.org. Web site: www.ers.org. Add the greater of $4.50 or 10% of total purchase price for shipping and handling. Phone orders accepted with Visa, MasterCard, or American Express.

Library of Congress Cataloging-in-Publication Data

Marx, Gary.
    An overview of sixteen trends, their profound impact on our future : implications for students, education, communities, and the whole of society / by Gary Marx.
    p. cm.
ISBN 1-931762-52-X
1. Education—Forecasting. 2. Educational planning. 3. Social prediction. 4. Forecasting. I. Marx, Gary. Sixteen trends, their profound impact on our future. II. Title.
LB41.5.M26 2006
370.9'05—dc22
                                                                              2006002688

About This Book

In 2000, Educational Research Service (ERS) published *Ten Trends: Educating Children for a Profoundly Different Future.* That book, which also included a companion *Overview*, was developed and written by Gary Marx. Assistance was provided by an ERS Schools of the Future Council and ERS staff. Since then, *Ten Trends* has become a valued resource used by thousands of educators as well as leaders in business, government, and the community at large. Educators in particular have drawn from that work in their efforts to ensure that schools and colleges are ready and able to address the future needs of students and society.

In a fast-changing world, education and other institutions must have ready access to updated projections and information about emerging trends. That is why Marx has written a new book, *Sixteen Trends... Their Profound Impact on Our Future: Implications for Students, Education, Communities, and the Whole of Society.* In developing that benchmark work, he has again enlisted the advice and assistance of a diverse and talented group of people, the Creating a Future Council of Advisors, to help him with this complex and important task.

This publication is an *Overview* of the *Sixteen Trends* book. Its purposes are to whet the appetite for even more information available through the larger work and to provide a vehicle for carrying basic information about trends and their implications to expanded numbers of people.

ERS extends its thanks to Gary Marx for taking on this important project. We hope that *Sixteen Trends*, both the book itself and this *Overview*, will be helpful to schools, colleges, governments, businesses, and communities worldwide as they face growing challenges on the road to the future.

About the Author

Gary Marx is president of the Center for Public Outreach, in Vienna, Va., an organization he founded in 1998, which provides counsel on future-oriented leadership, communication, education, community, and democracy.

Prior to launching the Center, Marx served for nearly 20 years as a senior executive for the American Association of School Administrators (AASA), as executive editor of more than 150 education leadership publications, and as a local school administrator. Marx was presented the coveted President's Award by the National School Public Relations Association (NSPRA) in 1999 and the Distinguished Service Award by AASA in 2000.

As an international speaker, workshop leader, and consultant, Marx has worked with education, community, business, association, and government leaders at all levels on four continents and in all 50 states. As a futurist, he has directed studies such as *Preparing Students for the 21st Century* (1996), *Preparing Schools and School Systems for the 21st Century* (1999), *Ten Trends . . . Educating Children for a Profoundly Different Future* (2000), *Future-Focused Leadership: Preparing Schools, Students, and Communities for Tomorrow's Realities* (2006), and *Sixteen Trends . . . Their Profound Impact on Our Future* (2006), the basis for this *Overview*.

Marx resides in the Washington, D.C. area and can be reached by phone, (703) 938-8725, or email, gmarxcpo@aol.com.

Contents

Introduction

We have a choice. We can simply defend what we have . . . or create what we need.

"A funny thing happened on the way to accomplishing our plan. The world changed."

Sound familiar? That's why strategic plans, no matter how sophisticated, need to become living strategies or strategic visions.

Defending the status quo has never been very exciting anyway. The excitement comes when we decide to create the future we need, not simply defend what we have. Unless we stay ahead of the curve, we'll fall behind. There is no more status quo. Change is inevitable, progress is optional.

To earn legitimacy, organizations need to be connected with the communities, countries, and world they serve. Unless they are constantly scanning the environment, educators and others in society will soon find themselves isolated . . . and out of touch.

Much of the future is unpredictable. However, as we scan the political, economic, social, technological, and other forces affecting our environment, a number of massive trends snap into focus. Like the movement of tectonic plates beneath the surface of the earth, these trends should serve as signals, since they have implications for schools, school systems, colleges, universities, and other institutions, including communities, nations, and the world.

The trends featured in this publication were identified with assistance from the Creating a Future Council of Advisors. Members of this diverse group, made up of representatives from education, business, government, and other fields, were asked to identify significant trends and issues that might affect education and society in the early part of the 21st century. They also speculated on possible implications of those trends. The Council's ideas were coupled with extensive reviews of trends and issues identified by futurists, forecasters, demographers, leadership experts, educators, governmental and nongovernmental agencies, international organizations, and many others.

This *Overview* is meant to be used in conjunction with the more expansive book on which it is based, *Sixteen Trends...Their Profound Impact on Our Future*. That book, which includes detailed information about each trend and suggestions for future-oriented planning, is designed to stimulate the planning process, encourage breakthrough thinking and risk taking, and clear the way for conceiving of a vision of what the future can become. We urge leaders everywhere to place these books in the hands of educators, parents, and others in the community.

Consider these trends just the tip of the iceberg; the list is by no means complete. There are many other trends that will have an impact on education, communities, and the whole of society. Our hope is that the information presented here will lead to a more expansive discussion and get us on the superhighway toward creating an even brighter future.

*For the first time in history, the old
will outnumber the young.*

*Worldwide: In developed nations, the old will substantially
outnumber the young. In underdeveloped nations,
the young will substantially outnumber the old.*

Younger → Older   Older → Younger

The handwriting is on the wall. In 2000, 27 percent of the U.S. population was 18 or younger, and 21 percent was 55 or older. By 2030, when the Baby Boom Generation is between 66 and 84 years of age, 25 percent will be 18 or younger, and 30 percent will be 55 or older.[1]

Why are the United States and other developed nations getting older? The answer is directly connected to the balance among six key factors:

• In 1789, *life expectancy* in the United State was about 35. By 2001, it had reached 77.2, according to the National Center for Health Statistics.[2] A child born in 2001 is expected to live 29.9 years longer than a child born in 1900.[3]

• In 1800, the *average age* of people in the United States was 16.[4] By 2000, that figure had more than doubled to 36.5. The U.S.

Census Bureau predicts an average age of 40.7 in 2050 and 42.1 in 2095.[5] Admittedly, no one knows for sure what breakthroughs in extending life, cures for diseases, or natural or human-caused disasters might intervene.

• While life expectancies and average ages continue their relentless climb, U.S. *birth rates* have taken a steady nosedive. In 1910, the United States registered 3.01 live births per 100 population.[6] In 1960, there were 2.37. By 1990, the rate had fallen to 1.67 and in 2002 dropped even further to 1.39.[7]

• In 2001, the *fertility rate* (the average number of live births per 100 women of normal childbearing age, 15 to 44) dropped to 6.53 from 7.09 in 1990. From 1946 to 1964, when the Baby Boomers were being born, the rates were substantially higher— 10.6 in 1950 and 11.8 in 1960.[8]

• In 2001, the United States reported a death rate of 8.5 per 1,000 population, compared with 14.7 in 1910.[9]

• A population factor that ameliorates the effect of all the others is *immigration*. While U.S. society is feeling its age, it is, on average, a bit younger than some developed countries, largely because of immigration. The U.S. Census Bureau reports that immigrants and their children accounted for 61 percent of the nation's population growth during the 1990s.[10]

■ Imbalances

While, on average, we're getting progressively older, the traditional school-age population is growing.

In Generations: By 2025, "the world's elderly population, ages 65 and above, will more than double, while the world's youth population, under age 15, will grow by six percent," according to U.S. Census Bureau's *World Population Profile*. The United States and most of the developed world will face "an elderly support burden nearly 50 percent larger in 2025 than it did in 1998."[11]

In contrast, most nations in the developing world will see massive increases in their youth populations but have few people older than 55. When there are huge numbers of young people who might be un- or under-educated and unemployed, with little obvious opportunity, anger grows. That anger can present itself in anything from an enlightened revolution to unending chaos, civil wars, and international terrorism.

In Education: In 2000, kindergarten through grade 12 enrollments in the United States stood at 53.16 million. Those numbers were expected to grow to 53.86 million by 2005 and then relax somewhat to 53.69 million in 2012, according to the National Center for Education Statistics (NCES).[12]

At the turn of the millennium, approximately 3.1 million people were part of the U.S. elementary and secondary teaching force. The number of teachers needed by 2008 was projected to increase to 3.46 million.[13]

■ Implications for Education

- **Balancing the political demands of the young and the old.** Ted Stilwill, former director of the Iowa Department of Education, warns of a possible "clash between the needs of those of us headed into retirement with the needs of young children for education and other services." Keith Marty, superintendent of the School District of Menomonee Falls in Wisconsin, comments, "School leaders and communities that collaborate and come together for children will be able to garner resources and public support" and better balance the political demands of the young and the old.

- **Recruiting and retaining older citizens for service as educators.** Growing enrollments expected during the early part of the 21st century will run squarely into massive retirements from education. The system must face head-on the problem of gaps created by retirements and movement from the profession.

- **Expanding career education, adult education, community and four-year college and university programs, and other opportunities for lifelong learning.** School systems and community colleges, as well as many four-year colleges and universities, have been working together in fits and starts to make the education system somewhat more seamless. Those efforts will likely be accelerated by the increasing demands of an aging population.

- **Promoting cross-generational communication.** Schools and colleges will be focusing on how to build services and constituencies across all or parts of five generations. At the same time, they will be considering how to prepare students for intergenerational understanding. For example, some schools may set aside part of the building as a senior center. Of course, meeting these needs involves policy, budgetary, and security issues.

- **Communicating with people who don't have kids in school.** Older citizens can be an education system's greatest gifts or its worst nightmares. If the more age-mature people in our communities have an opportunity to be engaged, they'll likely feel a sense of ownership. If contact is limited, battle lines could be drawn between the needs of older citizens and the needs of young people. That's why effective communication with citizens who do not have children in school is essential.

- **Maintaining the solvency of pension funds.** The growing phalanx of people poised for either early or on-time retirement, coupled with reduced return on pension fund investments, threats about cutbacks in Social Security, and the fact that people are living longer, has placed a growing strain on retirement systems. Education institutions can expect this ongoing issue to move to the critical list during the early decades of the 21st century.

*Majorities will become minorities, creating
ongoing challenges for social cohesion.*

Majority/Minority → Minority/Minority

*Worldwide: Growing numbers of people and
nations will discover that if we manage our
diversity well, it will enrich us. If we don't
manage our diversity well, it will divide us.*

Diversity = Division ←→ Diversity = Enrichment

The United States is becoming a nation of minorities. Shortly after
2050, no single racial or ethnic group will constitute more than 50
percent of the population.

- In 2000, 71.4 percent of the nation's 275.3 million people were
  non-Hispanic White. By 2050, 52.8 percent are likely to be in
  that category. In 2100, the number of non-Hispanic Whites is
  expected to drop to 40.3 percent. While Blacks and Native

As you study each of the trends, you might ask, "What's the difference between
→ and ←→?" The → mark indicates a clear, nearly unmitigated trend. A
designation of ←→ indicates a trend that can be expected to develop or continue
based on both evidence and the reality that certain conditions are likely unsustainable. For example, we can expect a tug between planetary security and self-interest,
and between polarization and open-mindedness.

Americans will show growth in numbers, they are expected to remain about the same as a percentage of the total population. Asians and Hispanics will increase dramatically.[14]

- The youth population in the United States, ages birth to 19, is projected to increase from 78.4 million in 2000 to approximately 106.4 million in 2050 and 144.6 million in 2100. While 64 percent of the 2000 youth population were non-Hispanic White, that number is expected to drop to 49.1 percent by 2040, 46.2 percent by 2050, and 34.4 percent by 2100.[15]

A number of factors are having a profound impact on turning the United States from a majority/minority into a minority/minority society. Some of the more prominent are:

- *Immigration.* In 2000, the total foreign-born population in the United States was approximately 31.1 million, a record 57 percent increase during the decade of the 1990s.[16] The country had a net immigration of 980,000 in 2000 alone. That number is now expected to decline to 757,000 in 2020, then increase to more than one million annually between 2028 and 2046.[17]

- *Birth rates.* Average birth rates vary among racial and ethnic groups. A 1998 report illustrated the discrepancies in rates among various groups: Whites averaged 1.23 children per 100 population, Asians 1.64, Blacks 1.82, and Hispanics 2.43. Over time, slight variations in those rates can have a profound impact on the total make-up of a population, locally, nationally, and worldwide.[18]

- *Multi-country nations.* Concentrations of wealth often bring lower birth rates and lower death rates. That means a good share of developed countries are aging, their labor forces dwindling. People of many races, cultures, and nations see these countries as "opportunity magnets." The tendency has been for people to move toward countries that feature market capitalism, political pluralism, and cultural diversity. In the global marketplace, people who come to work and raise their families in these types of countries don't necessarily want to give up their culture and connection to their homeland. In short, for growing numbers of people in the world, shared culture and history have become greater unifying factors than political boundaries. These people are becoming today's "quintessential cosmopolitans."[19] Let's face it, the people of "a nation" might actually live in many different countries.

If we accept diversity as part of the norm, it will enrich us, bind us together. If we don't, our diversity can divide us. Each community and nation, in an increasingly mobile world, will be challenged to constantly reframe its identity or face division, dissension, and lost potential.

■ Implications for Education

- **Improving achievement for *all* students.** Perhaps no other issue raised by this trend is so critical as making sure each and every student has an equal opportunity to receive a sound education. Challenges, even conflicts, will likely grow as some students and their schools fail to meet benchmarks on high-stakes tests. Public Advocacy for Kids' Arnold Fege comments that at least two types of students might suffer disadvantage, those who "do not experience success" and those who "do not have an opportunity to learn in diverse settings."

- **Providing inclusive, multicultural education.** Wherever students grow up, they ultimately will have to survive and thrive in a multicultural world, made even smaller by instant communication and rapid transportation. Betsy Rogers, 2003 U.S. National Teacher of the Year, declares that an education that helps students understand multiple cultures "must become a part of our curriculum K-12."

- **Pursuing social cohesion, seeking common denominators, and adjusting our identity.** While we are learning about and celebrating our diversity, we also need to help students, staff, and communities find common denominators. Many communities and their education systems will need to consider adopting new, even more inclusive, identities to match their evolving demographics. If they don't, they will lose their social cohesion.

- **Attracting and keeping excellent teachers and role models.** The percentage of minority students will continue to increase, but many education systems have been hard-pressed to adequately tap the talent pool of minority teachers and administrators to serve as role models for students. In an effort to fill the gap, some education systems are refocusing their recruitment efforts, encouraging members of minority groups to pursue careers in education, and even attracting teachers from other countries.

- **Helping students, parents, educators, and community members understand a rapidly changing world.** Students, parents, educators, and communities need to be prepared for the educational implications of a society that is becoming even more pluralistic and a world that is increasingly complex.

- **Insisting on preparation and professional development programs that address diversity.** We need to be sure that preparation programs at colleges and universities and professional development programs at local, state, national, and international levels change with the times. Everyone needs to understand how to work with students, staff, and communities in a highly diverse world.

- **Catching up with the students.** Growing numbers of students are ahead of the curve in understanding the need for an education that prepares them to constructively engage with people who might seem different from them. "Students will require adults to make a transition to the new minority/minority world," suggests Rosa Smith, president of the Schott Foundation in Cambridge, Mass.

- **Developing an international focus.** The student who is prepared for the future will need a grounding not just in the pop culture of his or her own country but in the histories, cultures, people, and languages of the world. All students, wherever they live, need a more global perspective.

- **Developing language and other communication skills.** Immigrant students, in varying degrees, are often fluent in more than one language. Rosa Smith recommends that all students eventually be required "to be fluent in at least three languages." She also notes that, in preparing for this international focus, schools will need updated and honest versions of world and American history and religions. Schools also need to continue to improve programs designed to help English language learners become successful in competitive school environments.

- **Becoming culturally sensitive.** C. Lynn Babcock, 2000 president of the National Association of Elementary School Principals, points out the challenge of dealing with "continued lack of understanding, acceptance, and tolerance of those who are different."[20] Education systems need to declare the importance of cultural sensitivity as a basic requirement for all educators.

- **Communicating effectively with the community.** To get the message to today's culturally diverse parents, schools need to consider everything from language to preferred media to the cultural weight of what is said. The same is true for listening as educators try to understand needs and deal with problems. Cultural sensitivity and effective communication go hand-in-hand.

- **Considering categories.** Lines of race and ethnicity have become blurred because of melding, melting, and mixing. The education system and society-at-large will feel continuing pressure to better understand that students might be a blend of several races, ethnicities, and cultures, and don't fit easily into any preconceived category.

• **Investing in all children.** We simply cannot afford to lose the talents, abilities, interests, and energies of any child anywhere in the world because of a lack of opportunity for education. Let's start by seeing education as a worthwhile investment that pays off, not as a mere expense.

Trend 3

Social and intellectual capital will become economic drivers, intensifying competition for well-educated people.

Industrial Age → Global Knowledge/Information Age

In "the good old days," most workers earned their living by the sweat of their brows and the strength of their backs. Today, although millions of people continue to strain their bodies to make a living, social and intellectual capital have become the prime sources of wealth in our new economy. Today, what you know and who you know both count.

Intellectual capital is "the intellectual material—the knowledge, information, intellectual property, experience—that can be put to use to create wealth."[21] Today, more and more people are discovering that this accelerating trend has a direct impact on their bottom line, in industries ranging from manufacturing cars to improving student achievement in schools. In business, competitive intelligence has become a major issue. Whatever our institution, we need to attract the best people we can and encourage them to think beyond what's currently on top of the desk.

Social capital depends on networks of social relationships that support success. "The problem facing almost all leaders in the future will be how to develop their organization's social architecture so that it actually generates intellectual capital."[22] Harvard Professor Robert Putnam placed social capital directly in the spotlight in his classic work, *Bowling Alone.* At a 2000 White House Conference on the New Economy, Putnam told a gathering of leaders, "The basic idea of social capital is that networks have value . . . for transmitting information . . . for undergirding cooperation and reciprocity."[23] Limit the circle, and you narrow the range of ideas that will refresh the organization. Broaden it, and intellectual wealth blossoms, paving the way for creating a future.

The future of any economy is tied directly to its ability to grow its social and intellectual capital. Setting the stage for the constant development of ideas and the free flow of information will be essential. Even today, knowledge workers constitute about 30 percent of the workforce but command about 50 percent of all wages and salaries. To secure a brighter future, communities are competing for these well-educated, creative people.

Schools and colleges have been in the intellectual and social capital business for a long time. What should be a major source of intellectual capital in every community? Where do we develop relationships that often last us the rest of our lives? The answer, of course, is "school!" The educational institution should be among the key venues where divergent people and ideas coalesce to form new knowledge.

■ Implications for Education

- **Preparing students for the future, not for the past.** Concern has grown that stringent standards and tests can create a box that actually inhibits the expansive education needed to thrive in a global knowledge/information age. Thinking and reasoning will be accepted as basic skills, not only for students, but also for teachers/professors and administrators.

- **Creating a new knowledge/information-based model for schools.** Today's schools were created to mirror the needs of an industrial society. What's needed is a system capable of preparing students for a global knowledge/information age. Considering that the world outside is moving at mind-bending speed, however, can schools and colleges make that change fast enough? The best possible scenario is that educational institutions will actually lead the change, using futures tools to help redefine themselves.

- **Getting students ready for the new economy.** People who are not prepared for an economy based on social and intellectual capital will stand a good chance of becoming "the new disadvantaged" in society. The skills and knowledge students will need include: basic management and entrepreneurial skills; the ability to collaborate with others; the ability to separate truth from fiction as they explore conflicting information that is expanding exponentially; critical and creative thinking skills; technological savvy; and an understanding of different cultural backgrounds. Add to that high levels of perseverance and curiosity; keen awareness of and sensitivity to the ethical dimensions of their discoveries, conclusions, and actions; and a full understanding of the principles of democracy, learned through civic education and actual practice.

- **Insisting on preparation and professional development that challenges habits and mindsets.** We need to be sure we are preparing not only aspiring teachers and administrators but also seasoned veterans to understand the implications of the knowledge/information age for them, their students, and their communities. Professional development programs will need to be frequent, with plenty of advice from thinkers and researchers and spirited peer-to-peer interaction, which is at the heart of a learning organization. Delivery will likely range from presentations and face-to-face interaction to online and other computer-assisted learning, including virtual reality.

• **Serving as a prime source of intellectual leadership for the community.** A credible intellectual leader sees things in context, understands both the big and little pictures, engages in both critical and creative thinking, and helps people understand not just what is happening but why it is meaningful and important. Every educator should make a commitment to becoming an intellectual leader. A good place to start is engaging staff and community in an informed discussion about how the education system and curriculum need to be shaped to effectively prepare students and the community for a new economy.

Technology will increase the speed of communication and the pace of advancement or decline.

Macro → Micro → Nano → Subatomic

One of the most newsworthy weddings in the history of our planet celebrated the marriage of computing and telecommunication. Those life-changing nuptials spawned an entirely new era. The sharing of information and creation of new ideas that may once have taken 80 years or more is now happening in eight minutes or eight seconds. In an interconnected world, educators, scientists, politicians, journalists, and people in general have access to instant information. We are connected to our home, our office, and the world by cell phones, headsets, pagers, global positioning systems, and an expanding number of personal digital assistants (PDAs). We can send and receive messages, hold cyber conversations, and explore a cascade of data and ideas at the click of a mouse or simply by hitting the "send" button.

What are the limits of technology? We don't really know. We do know this, however: Those schools and colleges, communities, businesses, and countries that make appropriate use of technology to help unleash the genius of their people will likely move forward at an unprecedented rate. Those that don't will likely fall backward at the same dizzying pace.

■ The Issue of Size

When ENIAC, (Electronic Numerical Integrator and Computer) first became operational in the mid-1940s, it filled an entire room; weighed 30 tons; had 19,000 vacuum tubes, 1,500 relays, and hundreds of resistors, capacitors, and inductors; and consumed 200 kilowatts of power. [24] As computers go, ENIAC would be *macro*.

Transistors and then silicon chips/microprocessors helped us go *micro*, to converge and miniaturize while increasing computer speed and capacity. Driving the economy of the future will be *nano*technology, which gives us the ability to manipulate atoms and molecules, promising stronger, lighter-weight materials than the world has ever known, faster computers, and unprecedented medical breakthroughs. And beyond nano? We're not there yet, but we're hearing more and more discussions of *subatomic* particles, neutrinos, and quarks.

■ Implications for Education

- **Capitalizing on the benefits of distance education.** Distance education is fast becoming an important part of the learning mix. For many smaller education systems, distance education has long been a source of programs that were hard to offer locally because of the lack of critical mass. Now, sources of distance learning range from computer networks and satellite communication to audio and video conferences and podcasts. Education systems and other organizations need to continue to select these programs wisely and provide professional development for everyone involved in how to use them most effectively.

- **Meeting the demand for higher-level teaching skills.** Growing numbers of students will come to school with more information on some topics than their teachers. As technologies increase student access to information, the teacher who is a subject-matter or grade-level specialist will also become a facilitator and orchestrator of learning, taking on a role as partner in the learning experience. "Teachers are becoming mentors and catalysts whose job is not to lecture, but to help students learn to collect, evaluate, analyze, and synthesize information."[25]

- **Making the school a learning community and a learning center for the community.** Schools will increasingly become centers of learning for their communities. Their Web sites will not only carry education information but also link to other community and worldwide sources, enabling students and parents to access learning resources, check on assignments, and get help with homework. "Technological advances in learning and telelearning will lead us toward redefining what we mean by learning communities, what we teach, and how we deliver education," says Kenneth Bird, superintendent of the Westside Community Schools in Omaha, Neb.

- **Opening the classroom to the world.** The examples are everywhere—from watching rovers traverse the surface of Mars to conversing with astronauts aboard the International Space Station or scientists probing the ocean depths. Students and teachers have been able to "go along for the ride" with scientists, archaeologists, and explorers. The challenge is to appropriately incorporate these widespread resources into curriculum and instruction.

- **Considering the implications of nanotechnology for education.** The people who will develop new products and services using nanotechnology are students in our schools and colleges today. Education systems need to think about the benefits of getting involved in nano at the ground floor. Consider, for example, a 2002 report in *Newsweek* magazine estimating a need for 800,000 to one million nanotechnology workers in the United States alone. The article also reported that the National Science Foundation (NSF) was requiring its six university nanotech centers to sponsor K-12 outreach programs.[26]

- **Investing in science education.** To stay ahead of the curve, any community or country will need to ensure students have an understanding of and appreciation for science in its many forms. Those who are prepared for scientific careers will be drawn to areas of the country and world where they are encouraged to conduct their research and engage in development. All people should be grounded in a basic understanding of science so that they can make reasoned judgments about budgetary allocations or the benefits and possible consequences of scientific projects.

- **Offering preparation and professional development that breaks habits and mindsets.** While computer power doubles on the average of every 18 months, some say that organizational change can take up to 20 years. That challenge hits home for many education institutions, especially since they are charged with preparing their students for the future. Preparation and professional development programs should focus on how to adapt quickly to new opportunities posed by technology.

- **Teaching the ethical dimensions of technology.** Technology can help us develop new generations of mind-bending processes and devices, such as the quantum computer. It can help us conquer diseases and make it possible for us to instantly exchange messages with someone half a world away. Intentionally or unintentionally, it can also help us spread diseases, wage attacks, and engage in online bullying and sexual harassment. Educators and students desperately need a solid grounding in the ethical dimensions of technology in what has become a very fast-moving world.

- **Discovering technologies to assist in both instruction and administration.** All educational institutions are on a fast track as they try to stay ahead of the technological curve. While time and budget often get in the way, the demand is unrelenting to develop, adopt, adapt, and effectively use new generations of technology. Most are working overtime to help their constituencies understand the need for support.

- **Offering leading-edge career, technical, and vocational education.** Demand will continue to grow for knowledge workers. That's why schools and colleges need to prepare students to understand and more effectively use new and often sophisticated technologies. This type of education and training also helps students connect what they're learning with what is important in the outside world and encourages them to consider career possibilities. All students should be prepared to use their imaginations to conceive of new technologies that will have a positive impact on society in the future.

- **Encouraging the restructuring and redesign of schools.** Growing numbers of schools are changing their industrial age structures to meet the needs and opportunities posed by the global knowledge/information age. Updates of the school facility should make way for state-of-the-art technologies that help improve the learning environment and connect schools with the community and the world. Air quality, acoustics, temperature, humidity, and lighting can be controlled to enhance rather than interfere with learning and to improve overall indoor environmental quality.

The Millennial Generation will insist on solutions to accumulated problems and injustices, while an emerging Generation E will call for equilibrium.

GIs, Silents, Boomers, Xers → Millennials, Generation E

Generational experts don't always agree on the exact span of years that defines each generation, nor do they fully agree on what to call them. They do, however, agree that there are certain core values that make one generation different from another. The actual characteristics are sharpened by human events.

At any time, four or five generations live side by side in our communities and on the planet. They often march to different drummers. That creates challenges for anyone who hopes to build understanding or consensus among people who have vastly different collections of life experience. Yet, keen observers such as William Strauss and Neil Howe note that every fourth generation tends to repeat itself, or at least exhibit significant similarities.[27]

Members of the Millennial Generation, born from about 1982 through 2003, have been in our elementary and secondary schools since 1987. The first of them graduated from high school and headed off to a job or college in about 2000. Generational experts tell us that, as a group, Millennials, much like the GI Generation four generations earlier, will be committed to solving the problems of the world and dealing with the injustices. People who study them tell us they are informal, self-reliant, street smart, technologically literate, practical, and accepting of diversity.

The parents of these Millennials are generally Baby Boomers, born between 1946 and 1964, or Generation Xers, born between 1965 and 1981. The Boomers, of course, will have a huge impact on pension systems as they start retiring in droves.

Beginning in about 2004, we began seeing the emergence of Generation E. "E" stands for equilibrium. As a group, the Es will probably be neither conservative nor liberal. In fact, they might blanch at the very thought of polarization, when civic discourse is so much more productive. In a 21st-century context, they'll try to cut the losses and consolidate the gains we've made during the previous four generations. They'll be showing up in kindergarten in about 2009 or 2010 and college in about 2022.

As the world takes its breath, the Es will likely spawn a new era for politics and world affairs, education, the environment, the arts, and culture, much of it beyond our imaginations. Part of their duty will be to explain us to ourselves, much as the "Silents" did four generations earlier, and to launch us on another generational mission of discovery.

■ Implications for Education

- **Helping students, educators, and communities understand divergent views.** Combined, the students, teachers, administrators, and parents who are directly involved in a school or college could represent up to three or four generations. Unless schools and colleges encourage cross-generational communication and understanding inside and outside their organizations, they should expect misunderstandings and even conflict.

• **Teaching students how to make change peacefully and democratically.** The Millennials, as they move into positions of leadership at every level, will take on the problems and injustices of the world. They will have some very destructive weapons at their disposal. Bottom line—Millennials will need to know how to channel their substantial energies constructively rather than destructively. Important knowledge and skills will include: thinking and reasoning skills; a sound code of ethics and an understanding of the value of others' opinions; practice in identifying and exploring issues, involving people in developing solutions, and drafting and promoting changes in public policy; and an ability to find and use information, communicate effectively, test ideas, and rally support through personal persuasion.

• **Developing student teamwork and management skills.** The Millennial Generation is committed to building what it considers a more just society. Educators will be pressed to offer what a recent study called "a curriculum for life that engages students in addressing real world problems, issues important to humanity, and questions that matter."[28] Project-based learning and teamwork will become prime motivators for these students. Distinguished futurist Joseph Coates believes "systems thinking aimed at helping students understand problems and possible solutions should be a core of teaching from kindergarten through college."

• **Helping students understand their roles in the global community.** Millennials may be the first generation in a century or two "to grow to adulthood in a world environment that is less centered on the United States," according to international relations veteran Frank Method of the Research Triangle Institute, International. Millennials will need a firm understanding of the histories, cultures, and people of the world, and the ability to become constructive citizens of a planet that extends beyond their national boundaries.

- **Listening to students ... giving them a voice.** This animated, energetic, committed generation of students will expect their voices to be heard in decisions that affect their education and their individual and collective futures. Listening to students is not just a nice thing to do. They have good ideas. They'll feel a greater sense of ownership. And it is *their* future.

- **Offering opportunities for intergenerational communication.** Consensus might seem elusive with so many generations having access to a world of information. Schools, school systems, colleges, and other organizations need to deliberately create opportunities for intergenerational communication. Advisory councils, targeted emails, newsletters, and "bring a grandparent to lunch day" will help. Conversations with Millennials leave the impression that they feel a sense of responsibility for shaping the future and, if given a safe opportunity, would like very much to exchange ideas with people who are older and have substantial life experience.

- **Building media literacy skills.** In a fast-moving world, often driven more by technology than values, we need guidelines as we think about what deserves consideration. We need to help students understand the difference between fact and fiction, information and disinformation, true and false. That's true whether we're making personal, family, or societal decisions ... or deciding what should show up in that end-of-semester term paper.

- **Helping students understand how to build a case.** As students pursue a cause, they need to know how to logically build a case. Their agility in mining the Internet can be helpful. On the other hand, they need to know how to organize their ideas, using creative and critical-thinking skills. Education will become even more exciting as students have an opportunity to regularly analyze and synthesize what they are learning. In the process, they are likely to develop new knowledge and engage in what leadership experts call breakthrough thinking.

- **Building an understanding of ethical behavior.** All institutions, including schools and colleges, will be held to high ethical standards. What is simply pragmatic or expedient will give way to the ethical—trying to determine the right thing to do. Staff will need training, and students will need to develop an understanding of ethics as we move into the post-Enron world.

- **Attracting Millennials into education careers.** If, indeed, members of the Millennial Generation want to make a positive impact on the future, they should consider careers in education. As teachers and administrators who are Boomers retire, the United States alone will need to attract more than two million new teachers to the nation's classrooms. The same type of scenario is playing out in countries around the world. Education systems need to focus attention on this high calling.

Standards and high-stakes tests will fuel a demand for personalization in an education system increasingly committed to lifelong human development.

Standardization → Personalization

More and more schools and students are being declared failures because they haven't measured up on high-stakes tests. Students are held back or not allowed to graduate. Young people are raising concerns that the education they're receiving has been narrowed, primarily to what is being tested—that it does not offer the depth and breadth they need to get into college or pursue their dreams. Many parents are beginning to worry that their children are not getting the personal attention they need to be prepared for the future.

Demand for personalization seems to be growing. The acceleration of interest, to some extent, is in direct reaction to the lack of flexibility in demands for students to demonstrate they have met certain standards by doing well on high-stakes tests. The problem with a one-size-fits-all approach is that each student is unique. These are not cookie-cutter kids. Round pegs don't fit into square holes, but that doesn't mean we don't need round pegs.

Newton's law is at work: To any action, there is an equal and opposite reaction. The outcome of the standards movement likely will be an increased demand for personalization of education. In a world crying for creative, knowledgeable people who've had an opportunity to develop their multitude of talents and abilities, what could be more positive?

We have a choice. Our standards can be narrow or expansive; they can be static or flexible. In education, they can freeze the system and its curriculum in the past, or they can encourage a constant process of preparing students for a future that is beyond our imagination.

■ Implications for Education

- **Personalizing as a key to reaching standards.** Schools will be challenged to shape education programs that balance the interests, abilities, talents, and aspirations of students with the needs of society. Since students have a world of information and ideas at their fingertips in our fast-emerging global knowledge/information age, they will insist on understanding why what they are expected to learn will be useful to them. We live in an era of mass customization, which constantly puts pressure on what we really mean by standardization. Educators and public officials need to realize the only logical way to reach and exceed appropriate standards will be through personalization. Some ask, "Can we afford it?" The answer may be found in another question, "What is the release of human genius worth as we move into the future?"

- **Ensuring standards do not limit the curriculum or push students out of school.** Average test scores will likely rise if we teach only a couple of things and forget everything else. However, students cannot be considered well educated if the curriculum is narrowed to only those few things that are tested and reported on the front page of the newspaper. Another way to raise test scores is to acquiesce, as students who are having problems drop out of school. Remember, however, that by 2030, only two people will be working for every person drawing benefits from Social Security. Those "people" had better be well educated and make a good living if we hope to have them paying Social Security taxes. Our individual and collective futures are at stake in making sure students stay in school and that their full range of talents is developed.

- **Linking equity and adequacy of funding.** Michael Silver, assistant professor of education at Seattle University and a veteran superintendent, notes, "For the last 50 years, since *Brown v. Board of Education*, the primary focus of schools and school finance has been to provide equal opportunity for students with limited resources." He adds, "With an increasing high-needs student population coupled with a set of common standards and assessment measures of quality education, the focus of school funding shifts from equity to adequacy."

- **Clarifying the limits of testing.** Education institutions may need to launch concerted communication programs aimed at building better community-wide understanding of the benefits and limits of testing.

- **Developing mutual expectations.** What expectations does a community, state, or country have for its schools? What expectations should the schools have for their communities, their governors and state legislators, their state and federal education agencies, the Congress, and the president? What expectations do we all have for students, and what are the expectations students should have for all of us? What we need are mutual expectations. It's not enough to declare expectations for others and then abandon ship.

- **Employing more performance-based testing.** Testing should provide students with an opportunity to show what they've learned. On the other hand, tests should provide educators with an indication of what students still need to learn. Performance-based testing often uses portfolios and exhibits of student work.

It allows students to demonstrate what they've learned in a number of ways. Teachers are, in many cases, more likely to understand what a student has mastered and where the student needs additional help from this type of performance-focused testing than from a fill-in-the-bubble multiple choice test that is, admittedly, easier to machine score.

• **Developing the individual talents and abilities of *all* students.** Whatever their social or economic backgrounds, all students should have an equal opportunity—and the encouragement—to flourish. However, some are concerned this type of personal or individual approach is inhibited by an overemphasis on *externally imposed* standards. To enhance the talents and abilities of each student, educators will need to consciously consider learning styles, strengths, weaknesses, and strategies for releasing each student's genius.

• **Encouraging educators to focus on preparing students for the future rather than acting merely as compliant bureaucrats.** Some educators express concern that they have little time for creating the education system their community needs, because they are too busy managing compliance with mandates. Whatever programs are mandated, educators need to see it as their duty to build on them to prepare students for life in a new millennium. Arnold Fege raises concern about what he sometimes sees as "the transformation of education leaders in our country from intellectual icons of their community to bureaucrats who are increasingly just a part of the infrastructure." He calls for educators to "transform education from the industrial model, characterized by efficiency, to the knowledge model, characterized by effectiveness that depends on the quality of educational, political, private sector, and community leadership."

Release of human ingenuity will become a primary responsibility of education and society.

Information Acquisition → Knowledge Creation and Breakthrough Thinking

"In 500 years, we've moved from a world where everything was certain and nothing changed to a world where nothing seems certain and everything changes."[29]

Nations are advancing and economies developing not by digging in their nails and hanging on to the status quo but by constantly creating new knowledge. A fresh generation of intellectual entrepreneurs is putting the pieces together, seeing certain things in a whole new light, dealing with paradox and controversy, developing creative solutions to problems, and conceiving of new knowledge-based industries.[30] Richard Florida, author of *The Rise of the Creative Class*, calls it "the 'Eureka' step."[31]

As we move at rocket speed into a global knowledge/information age, we are confronted by unprecedented progress, accompanied by a startling number of real and possible side-effects, wildcards, and both intended and unintended consequences. It's a time of reinvention. Every institution, including our education system, will be renewed. Either we can take the lead to engage people in that renewal, or others will do the renewing for us.

Why should educators be concerned? The reasons are crystal clear. First, in addition to delivering prescribed information and building skills, they'll be expected to recognize and release the genius that is already there. Second, they'll be expected to prepare students to become good citizens who are employable and well-adjusted people, capable of shaping an even brighter future.

■ Implications for Education

- **Helping students learn across disciplines.** While the standards movement makes many teachers and administrators cautious about focusing on the white spaces between disciplines, these educators will need to overcome their apprehension. Look at a person who is truly well educated and wise, and you'll discover a person who sees connections.

- **Applying what we know from cognitive research.** Perhaps more than anything else, the brain makes connections. As educators, we need to give it things to connect. Emotion, says Edward O. Wilson, is what "animates and focuses mental activity." He adds, "Without the stimulus and guidance of emotion, rational thought slows and disintegrates." Certainly, educators need to apply what they have learned from studies of multiple intelligences.[32] Prime questions to ponder: How can we make schools more interesting for all students? How can we help our students develop a broad range of interests, ideas, and skills, and learn how to connect the dots?

- **Making thinking and reasoning basic to education.** Students need to be nurtured in both critical and creative thinking. On the one hand, they need to understand syllogistic logic, inductive and deductive reasoning, and how to use it. On the other hand, educators need to cultivate students' and their own capacities for lateral or creative thinking, flashes of insight, and thinking outside the box. One more thing: Let's not lose their imagination. Albert Einstein, in fact, argued, "Imagination is more important than knowledge." Courage will be needed, especially when budgets are tight, to encourage the dreams and rescue the ingenuity of even those we consider—or who consider themselves—unimaginative.

- **Helping students turn data and information into usable knowledge and knowledge into wisdom.** The teacher should celebrate whenever a student has mined the Internet, cracked the books, and discovered new knowledge. In a fast-track, connected world, teachers should also enjoy using their own higher-level skills and life experiences to help students turn raw data and information into usable knowledge. Then, in many cases, teachers will help nudge students toward wisdom, building an understanding of "what that knowledge means for us personally, for our school, our community, our country, and the world."

- **Asking if what students have learned has triggered any ideas.** To send a message to students that knowledge doesn't stop with the last version of our lecture notes, try something like this: "Think about what we've studied today—what we've discussed. Does that trigger any ideas for you?" At the end of the class, the world will be smarter than when class got under way. In the process, students will be able to pool what they've learned in class, their life experience, and their insights, as they create new knowledge and engage in breakthrough thinking.

- **Emphasizing the arts as a way to create, express, and think across disciplines.** The arts, in their many forms, are a discipline in themselves. On the other hand, music, dance, musical theater, the visual arts, creative writing, and design appeal to a diversity of people and help to express or capture common ground across all disciplines. The arts can also help us teach other subjects, ranging from math to history.

- **Integrating the curriculum and helping students understand connections.** "Learning across disciplines can help move us from knowledge for its own sake to an understanding of how that knowledge can be used," according to technology leader Willard Daggett.[33] Forming connections has many benefits: building an understanding of relevance and meaning, engaging students through active learning, focusing the program to meet the needs and interests of various learners, and providing an opportunity for educators to build synergy by sharing ideas and techniques across disciplines. A commitment to integrating the curriculum and building connections can move any organization, but especially a school or college, from static to dynamic.

- **Moving toward intellectual leadership.** As we enter the new millennium, we are coming to the stark realization that no matter how well managed an institution might be, it will very likely be lost without visionary leadership. People with vision are able to connect disparate ideas. They are able to explain the implications of a proposal or a decision for numerous groups of real, live people. Courageous visionary leaders are eager to bring people from many disciplines together in the hope of seeing problems or opportunities in a whole new light.

- **Offering gravity-breaking preparation and professional development programs.** We need to help students turn information into knowledge and knowledge into wisdom. That means educators need these same skills. Both in teaching and in leading, educators need gravity-breaking preparation and professional development programs that go beyond mechanics. Nuts and bolts are important, but we also need to be prepared to apply our thinking and reasoning skills as we plan and work across disciplines, departments, and community, state, national, and international issues and organizations.

- **Helping students understand 21st-century interdisciplinary careers.** Students should have a grasp of the opportunities popping up in interdisciplinary industries such as bioinformatics. They also need to know they are the ones who will develop the interdisciplinary industries and careers of the future.

- **Making futures studies an essential part of education.** To excite students' interest, ask them to consider alternative futures and plan backward from the outcomes they'd like to see. Futures studies, as a course, a unit, or simply incorporated into nearly every discipline, stimulates critical and creative thinking skills, promotes active learning, and encourages students to develop their visions.

- **Teaching social responsibility.** In a post-Enron world, all organizations and students need to understand the importance of corporate citizenship and social responsibility. As members of the Millennial Generation move into positions of leadership, they will need to be armed with thinking and reasoning skills and the power to explore connections. As leaders in education, we need to engage broad groups of people inside and outside the system to help us think through our social responsibility, because schools have a massive impact on any community and on our individual and collective futures.

Trend 8

Continuous improvement will replace quick fixes and defense of the status quo.

Quick Fixes/Status Quo → Continuous Improvement

People today expect and demand quality, effectiveness, and service. In the past, an organization might get by with defending the status quo or going for the quick fix—the band-aid approach. Now, in an impatient world, people want products and services that work, meet their needs, and are delivered on time.

Continuous improvement should be one of the prime values embedded in the culture of any type of institution, including government, business, and education. In fact, a commitment to becoming even better tomorrow than we are today is a key to survival, maybe even a moral imperative.

How can we move from defining success based on our ability to defend the status quo and keep the world at bay, on the one hand, to the constant and exciting process of creating a future, on the other? Let's face it. If we were perfect yesterday, we probably aren't perfect today, because the world changed overnight. The question is: Are we flexible enough to adjust?

In probing continuous improvement, noted leadership consultant Rowan Gibson asks, "How will the 21st century organization develop a sense of foresight about where it needs to be heading? How will it create a meaningful vision and purpose; a goal that is uniquely its own, and that will give it a sustainable competitive advantage; something that it can stand for in a crowded and confusing world?" His answer: leadership.

Gibson adds that these leaders "will be looking forward, scanning the landscape, watching the competition, spotting emerging trends and new opportunities, avoiding impending crises. They will be explorers, adventurers, and trailblazers."[34]

■ Implications for Education

- **Putting the status quo to rest.** *Preparing Schools and School Systems for the 21st Century*, a study released at the turn of the century by the American Association of School Administrators, says continuous improvement should be "a driving force in every school and school system…. Educators cannot let the system stiffen or become atrophied in our fast-changing world."[35] Governing boards, administrators, teachers, and the communities they serve will all be key players in making sure the system becomes even better tomorrow than it is today.

- **Developing and adopting a continuous improvement process.** Early attempts at incorporating total quality management may have proven ungainly for many education systems. Growing numbers of institutions in education, business, and government, however, have been working through the process to make it more user-friendly. Continuous improvement is a constantly moving bull's eye. Organizations can readily learn from the experiences of others, select from the volumes of books and articles on the topic, review Baldrige Award materials, seek counsel, and get on with this exciting process.

- **Incorporating quality and continuous improvement into the classroom.** In some classrooms, students are actually schooled on the principles of continuous improvement. It's part of how the learning process works. They enthusiastically point out how their lessons and their personal goals are aligned with the aims of the school system. As they monitor their progress, they confer with other students who may need help with a concept or who might be able to help them. These students, playing a key role as managers of their own learning, work in teams.

- **Earning the opportunity to serve.** Organizations take up space. They are there because they've accepted the responsibility for providing what they hope will be an essential cluster of services. They create value. With lightning-speed communication, however, competition has grown. Others may want to occupy that space. That's why any organization, including an education system, must constantly prove to its constituencies that it is providing value and earning the opportunity to serve.

- **Using continuous improvement as a springboard for constant renewal.** Perhaps one of the greatest values of continuous improvement—the one that constantly pumps new life into an organization—is the belief that we're never finished. "A teacher's real commitment to continuous learning is noticeable when it's present and when it's not," observes Rowe, Inc., President Gary Rowe. "An improving school has teachers who are always talking about new things, new ideas, new concepts in the disciplines they are teaching, and they're actively sharing information with each other."

- **Bringing community and staff on board.** Getting people involved in the pursuit of better education will increase the social and intellectual capital (knowledge and relationships) brought to the endeavor and will exponentially expand the sense of ownership. Involve staff, board, parents, non-parent taxpayers, and students, as well as representatives of colleges and universities, businesses, and other units of government. Engage non-governmental organizations, consultants, professional and trade associations, and respected community leaders in the process of understanding, conceiving of, and building support for continuous improvement.

• **Offering heads-up professional development.** Organizations are only as effective as their people. However, those people are increasingly eager to learn. In fact, generational experts remark that the opportunity to learn new things and build skills will be like a magnet for recruiting and keeping talented people who were just moving into education careers at the turn of the 21st century. On top of that, a commitment to continuous improvement requires an almost seamless operation, with people working together across disciplines and departments toward common goals.

• **Maintaining flexibility to deal with a fast-changing world.** Opportunities might pop up. Certain needs might grow. Interest in certain topics might virtually explode. Are we flexible enough to deal with what were once called distractions? In a multi-faceted world, we need to find exhilaration in working with at least some level of chaos.

Scientific discoveries and societal realities will force widespread ethical choices.

Pragmatic/Expedient → Ethical

Few decisions are all right or all wrong. Many involve the lesser of two evils. Constantly trying to do the right thing, however, is basic to a civil society.

A recent cascade of ethical breaches in business, sports, and the media has sparked renewed interest in ethics. Business schools are introducing or upgrading their ethics courses. More conferences are including an ethics component. Each day, television programs and newspaper and magazine articles point to ethical concerns in every walk of life. Our awareness has been heightened.

Incredible developments in science and technology, coupled with societal realities, are constantly pushing the ethical envelope. As we consider scientific discoveries, for example, we are faced with a virtual explosion of possible benefits that will inevitably be measured against their potential side effects or unintended consequences.

If we think and care about how our actions will affect our fellow human beings and our environment, we'll be on the road to making better decisions. Albert Schweitzer put it this way, "The first step in the evolution of ethics is a sense of solidarity with other human beings."

■ Ethical Issues Facing Today's Students

Can we truly say a student is well educated without a firm grasp of ethical behavior? Probably not. As they move into positions of leadership and take on their role as citizens, students who are in schools and colleges today will be faced with some of the most monumental ethical dilemmas of all time—all the more reason why they will need an understanding of how to consider the ethical dimension. A few of the issues they likely will face include:

- A world population expected to grow from approximately six billion in 2000 to nearly nine billion by 2050. That's about a 50 percent increase in 50 years. Already, about half of all people on Earth live on less than $2 per day, and approximately 1.3 billion people live on less than $1 per day.[36]

- Stewardship of the environment.

- The introduction of life forms that may not currently exist on other planets . . . or actual colonization.

- Crime and corruption.

- Genetically modified foods (GMFs) and genetically modified organisms (GMOs).

- Computer ethics, ranging from using the computer to pirate music and search other people's private files to hacking and implanting viruses, worms, or Trojans.

- Investments that are or are not made in seeking the cures for major diseases or pandemics.

- Clashes among cultures and civilizations as they vie for dominance.

- Violations of basic human rights.

■ Implications for Education

- **Modeling ethical leadership.** Education institutions, by their very nature, are expected to be paragons of ethical behavior, because they play such a central role in modeling that type of behavior for students. As issues are discussed, administrators, board members, and teachers have an opportunity to make the ethical dimension of their pending decisions a part of their discussions.

- **Including an ethics component in every course.** Following corporate scandals of the early 2000s, many colleges and universities—especially business schools—rushed to include or upgrade existing ethics courses. The ethical dimension should be addressed at *all* levels of education. In any class, daily or weekly, a teacher might present this challenge, "Think about what we've discussed. What are the ethical implications for us as individuals, for our school, for our community, for our country, for the world?"

- **Expanding programs in thinking and reasoning skills as well as civic and character education.** As students develop their critical and creative thinking skills, they will be better prepared to observe the pros and cons as they make choices and solve problems, whether in school, on the job, or as citizens on the front lines of society. Civic education provides students with a grounding in how the system works and how they might change it, peacefully and democratically. Character education might focus on areas such as trustworthiness, respect, responsibility, fairness, caring, and citizenship.

- **Offering professional development to build a capacity to teach about ethics.** Not everyone has developed the knowledge and skills to effectively teach an ethics course. Most educators, however, can readily understand how to include a compelling ethics component in their courses, whatever their disciplines.

- **Making the school system an ethical resource for the community.** Of all institutions, schools and colleges are expected to take the higher ground. With their intellectual integrity, they can become a unifying force in their communities. For example, schools might offer advice and counsel as community and business organizations develop their codes of ethics and deal with ethical dilemmas. Ethical skills are fast becoming survival skills.

Common opportunities and threats will intensify a
worldwide demand for planetary security.

Personal Security/Self-Interest ⟷ *Planetary Security*

Common Threats ⟷ *Common Opportunities*

We are the first generations of people who have the capacity to destroy the world . . . and we may be the last generations that are capable of saving it. What happens will depend largely on how well we educate our people.

Students who are in our schools and colleges today will be expected to develop the ideas, techniques, and technologies to sustain our planet.

Unless those students have some understanding of the issues they confront, they may have difficulty dealing with them. Unless they understand that our personal interest, self-interest, or corporate interest means nothing if we destroy the biosphere in pursuing it, they may miss one of the connections fundamental to our very survival.

What about the sense of urgency? In 2005, "The most comprehensive analysis ever conducted of how the world's oceans, dry lands, forests, and species interact and depend on one another" reached a dramatic conclusion. A total of 1,300 authors from 95 countries participated in this Millennial Ecosystem Assessment. One of their conclusions: "Human actions are depleting Earth's natural capital, putting such strain on the environment that the ability of the planet's ecosystems to sustain future generations can no longer be taken for granted."[37]

The population of our planet is growing exponentially. Between 2000 and 2050, for example, the Earth's population is expected to grow 50 percent, from six billion to about nine billion people. Each of those nine billion will be born with a hierarchy of human needs ranging from oxygen, food, water, and a fairly constant body temperature to a sense of safety and security. As competition increases to satisfy self-interest and ensure personal security, the haves will increasingly be pitted against the have-nots. Technologies, devised to improve the quality of life, will also be used for terrorism and to wage wars.

While we're turning out good citizens for our communities and our nations, we also need to be sure we're producing good citizens of the world, or the world will start closing in on us.

■ Implications for Education

- **Balancing economic development and environmental sustainability.** As we make progress in our communities, in our nation, and globally, we need to measure what we do against its impact on our environment and the legacy we leave for future generations. In the short run, an unsustainable activity might make a few people much richer. In the long run, it might make all of us much poorer. "Schooling will have an increased focus on the science and ethics of environmental issues," predicts Ted Blaesing, superintendent of the White Bear Lake Area Schools in Minnesota. Blaesing also sees "environmentally friendly" school buildings. "Green schools—located to minimize transportation of students to the building —will be the norm."

- **Considering the impact of globalization.** "Globalization has the paradoxical effect of simultaneously increasing human interconnection and decreasing human physical security," observes the Shoah Foundation's Douglas Greenberg. "Every great revolution in transportation and communication has had this perverse effect." Greenberg suggests we "think about the human consequences of Europeans figuring out how to navigate the Atlantic. It led to an epidemiological catastrophe in the form of smallpox epidemics and other diseases among the natives of the Americas, and it also made the slave trade possible." Greenberg submits, "Only education on a massive and global scale can stand effectively against the array of dangers that confront us."

- **Offering futures courses.** As students study futures, they will develop techniques for better understanding the social, political, economic, technological, and environmental forces that drive us today and the potential impact our decisions will have on related trends and issues tomorrow. Futurist Joseph Coates suggests development of "a curriculum around threats and remedies from the immediate to those we might face in 1,000 years or more." Through futures studies, students will become even more interested in learning about natural and human forces affecting their communities and the planet. Many will discover or even develop careers for dealing with those challenges.

- **Stimulating creativity.** Faced with gigantic issues and often skepticism or outright resistance to addressing them, students will need to develop their creativity. "Creativity needs to be more central to the learning process," according to Frank Method, an international relations veteran who is director of education policy for the Research Triangle Institute, International. Method suggests using "simulations, modeling, exploratory learning that can help open new possibilities, and the arts to help articulate feelings and visions not yet demonstrated in the reality that we've already faced."

- **Building media literacy skills.** "Media awareness and critical thinking skills need to be prominent in the preparation of learners," Method recommends. Students, he said, "need to understand the tendency of news media to conflate events and images and to extrapolate patterns from anecdotal data drawn from a large world. At the same time, they will need critical thinking skills to help them sort things that they can do something about from those that only tangentially affect their lives." Method adds that students will also need "values of resiliency, tolerance, and openness to change . . . balanced with strength and courage in the face of challenges." As they encounter information, whether in a book, online, or through personal conversations, students will need to be adept at distinguishing truth, fiction, fact, misinformation, disinformation, and propaganda.

- **Building an understanding of basic human needs.** In our schools and communities, we need to better understand ourselves and others. All of us need a better grasp of what motivates people and what people need, whether they live next door or on the other side of the planet.

- **Developing a philosophy of possibility.** In totalitarian regimes, one of the more frequent responses when people are presented with a suggestion is, "It is not possible." In more democratic societies, we are more likely to encounter the philosophy that "anything is possible." How we feel about possibility will play a huge role in charting our future. At its best, education and community leaders should instill a sense of possibility.

*Polarization and narrowness will bend toward
reasoned discussion, evidence, and
consideration of varying points of view.*

Narrowness ←→ Open-Mindedness

Today, we have what seems to be growing numbers of people whose righteousness has hardened their attitudes and limited their view. For some, everything is straightforward black or white. Shades of gray have disappeared. Rather than considering an idea or an opinion on its merits, many of us rush to reject the idea and discredit its source. "I'm right, and you're wrong. It's as simple as that." No discussion.

Polarization and narrowness play out inside families, friendships, and communities, and both within and among nations. Talk shows on radio and television are more often shouting matches than civil discussions. Web sites proliferate to justify a single, often narrow, point of view. Conspiracy theories abound.

Political candidates, and many who already hold elected or appointed office, confront the opposition rather than learn from it. Partisanship reigns, too often crushing bipartisanship and even principle, when the principle might possibly be the common good.

People declare themselves liberal or conservative and vow against all reason to justify the moniker they've adopted.

What's at stake with this way of thinking? The very future of a civil society.

A major driver of education is a commitment to prepare students to become engaged, contributing members of civil society. That should mean they understand the importance of reasoned discussion; they know how to gather, consider, and present evidence; and they have some commitment to comprehending, not necessarily accepting, a variety of points of view. A truly free and open society needs to be based on open-mindedness, not on an isolating form of narrowness. Students need to understand how they can most constructively function in that kind of intellectually rich environment.

■ Implications for Education

- **Prepare people to engage in reasoned discussion.** Whether in the classroom, a community organization, or in conversation with colleagues, friends, and fellow citizens, we need to practice civil discussion. Thoughtful people know that it is important to seek other opinions rather than simply filtering out any point of view other than our own. Of course, that doesn't stand in the way of having "strong feelings" or a "point of view." We're not talking about "going along to get along" or "caving in." Instead, we're making a case for civil discourse.

- **Offer courses that encourage thinking and reasoning and communication skills.** In a fast-changing world, especially in a democratic society, students should be prepared to do objective research. They should be media literate, capable of separating wheat from chaff, truth from fiction. Students need experience in engaging others in civil discussion and the communication skills they'll need to coherently present their case. All of the above are grounded in a belief that thinking and reasoning are basic skills.

- **Individuals, governments and institutions at all levels, and students need to develop an attitude and belief that polarization and narrowness can be overcome.** We have become so accustomed to escalating conflict that we sometimes don't realize how far it can escalate and how destructive it can be. Throughout history, wars have been fought over the conflict of ideas. More will likely follow, based on clashes along cultural and civilizational boundaries. However, as weapons have become more lethal, we're coming to realize that life on Earth may be the stakes we've placed on the table.

- **Students and other citizens will need to master the art of making change peacefully and democratically.** Constitutional democracies generally create a marketplace of ideas where a broad range of issues can be discussed. The First Amendment to the U.S. Constitution declares "Congress shall make no law respecting an establishment of religion, or prohibiting the free exercise thereof; or abridging the freedom of speech, or of the press, or the right of the people peaceably to assemble, and to petition the Government for a redress of grievances." A challenge for schools, colleges, and society-at-large will be to build a greater understanding of the implications of this amendment as we civilly deal with controversy.

As nations vie for understanding and respect in an interdependent world, international learning, including diplomatic skills, will become basic.

Sub-trend: To earn respect in an interdependent world, nations will be expected to demonstrate their reliability and tolerance.

Isolationist Independence ←→ Interdependence

National reputations . . . *They depend on each of us and all of us.*

The behaviors of governmental and non-governmental organizations, businesses, and individuals help shape national reputations. How people feel about a country depends on more than glowing words in a travel brochure. Policies and actions speak more loudly than words. Over time, national reputations become directly tied to the level of respect any country enjoys as a member of the community of nations. That level of respect could ultimately be a key to a country's success, even its survival.

Many people, including some educators, might dismiss the idea that national respect is related to education, believing that international relations is the government's business. While most people in nations around the globe do depend on their governments to handle macro-diplomatic issues, we can't escape individual responsibility. We are, after all, the ones who elect and/or tolerate the behavior of our governments.

It's time we realized that, wherever we are, whatever our line of work, we are affected by nearly everything else that's happening in the world. Students who leave school without some grounding in international education may turn out to be the new disadvantaged.

■ Implications for Education

• **International education will become basic.** The stakes are high and the possible benefits so great that schools and colleges will be expected to strengthen their international education programs. The United States and several other nations benefit from having students and educators in their schools from many parts of the world. Relationships that grow from international study and exchange programs foster understanding and an opportunity to develop appreciation, even admiration, for others. Educators and students will want to explore programs in diplomacy, international relations, global issues, conflict resolution, languages other than their own, and the histories and cultures of other parts of the world. International studies is also enhanced by a grounding in civics; economics; law; geography; history; political, arts, and character education; and an introduction to cultural anthropology. Social studies can help us develop a deeper understanding of issues close to home and an even more expansive view of the world.

What do we mean by diplomatic skills? Consider these: an open mind, natural curiosity, patience, courtesy and good manners, a sense of tolerance, and the ability to put oneself in someone else's shoes.

International relations expert Frank Method predicts "open information systems and networked learning will increasingly lead to dialogue and exchanges across political, economic, and social boundaries." He cautions, "These exchanges will not necessarily lead to agreement or comity. Young learners will need help managing these exchanges. Listening skills in framing/reframing questions and issues will be as important as debating and advocacy skills." Method notes students will also need skills in developing and respecting standards and values, and in defending ideals.

On the agenda for learning and discussion, Method suggests, might be principles underlying the development of international agreements, the resolution of disputes, setting international standards for acceptable practices, criminality, business law, accounting standards, food safety, environmental stewardship, human rights, and myriad other topics.

- **Society should be prepared to communicate and do business across international boundaries.** Growing numbers of companies have multinational owners. Today's students likely will work for and even lead many of these and other types of organizations. Education systems will be expected to turn out new generations of professional diplomats, but that might not be enough. Each of us, in a shrinking and fast-moving world, will very likely need a strong set of diplomatic skills.

- **Students could engage in discussions that result in what they consider a legitimate measuring stick, or criteria, for any country that hopes to become a respected member of the family of nations.** Taking the process a step further, students and communities could expand their conversation to consider the impact of those criteria on future national or even local goals. White Bear Lake (Minn.) Superintendent Ted Blaesing, looks ahead to "students of all ages increasingly traveling as part of their normal course of study and certainly connecting with each other via the latest technology." He expresses concern, however, about working an international curriculum into an already crowded school day, largely focused on state and federal requirements. Blaesing also sees international implications for school policy. "I can foresee a school district policy that might read in part, 'all products will be purchased by the school district from manufacturers and companies that offer economic justice to workers,'" he states.

- **Professional development programs will provide educators with a grounding in international education.** Some educators travel and try to understand and appreciate the histories, cultures, and peoples of the world. Nonetheless, few have been able to explore the range of possibilities for incorporating an international perspective into courses ranging from math to social studies and the arts.

- **Demand will grow for continuing education programs that focus on international issues and opportunities.** Students will increasingly understand that they will need to be able to live, work, and thrive in a multitude of cultures and locations world-wide. People of all ages and walks of life are likely to demand expanded opportunities to learn about other people and nations through college, university, online, and adult education courses.

- **Community, business, and civic leaders increasingly will build relationships with counterparts in other nations.** While students pursue internationally oriented projects, communities might develop relationships through programs such as Sister Cities; host festivals celebrating the richness of the many cultures that comprise their areas; encourage participation in programs such as the Peace Corps; sponsor student, educator, and other community exchange programs; and pursue business relationships with people in other nations. Both students and their communities should consider the international benefits and consequences, both intended and unintended, that could result from various proposals for economic and other types of development.

Greater numbers of people will seek personal
meaning in their lives in response to an intense,
high-tech, always on, fast-moving society.

Personal Accomplishment ←→ *Personal Meaning*

Early in the 2000s, two major business magazines, *Fortune* and
Kiplinger's, carried cover stories on the need people were feeling to step
back from the frenzy and seek spiritual renewal.[38] Those stories reflect
what many identify as a growing frustration with being wired, acces-
sible at all hours of day and night, working 24/7, and seeing the
consequences for their families and their own personal interests.

"Most people are in a rut, doing what they are expected to rather than
what they want to do," Kirstin Davis and Mary Beth Franklin noted in
their *Kiplinger's* article. They kick off their timeless piece with this
statement, "You've heard it all your life: Time is money. But a growing
number of Americans are deciding that the relentless pursuit of money
is leaving them too little time to enjoy it. They are stepping back from
their fast-paced, workaholic lifestyles and making changes to bring
more balance into their lives, carving out more time for their families
and passions—even when it means making do with less."[39]

We can expect that, in addition to looking outward, even more
people will be looking inward to personal relationships—as the

physical and emotional foundation that supports them. Rather than being satisfied with lowest common denominators, they'll aspire to highest common possibilities.

■ Implications for Education

• **Considering how business, government, education, and other institutions can contribute to work-life balance.** There are at least two rules. First, we need to understand that it's OK to unwire long enough to unwind and refresh. Second, we need to know how. Some people have been so busy for so long that they either feel guilty or have no idea what to do when they are presented with leisure time. Michael Silver, assistant professor of education at Seattle University and a veteran superintendent, foresees an expansion of school curriculum to provide students with a greater number of humanities and arts courses of study, helping them learn how to build relationships and reach out to others for friendship and collaboration, and making a search for identity an interdisciplinary theme for middle and high school courses. "A sustainable world cannot be built without full engagement of the human spirit," says Gary Gardner, director of research for the Worldwatch Institute.[40] The quest is on for purposeful lives and meaningful legacies.

• **Attracting more young people and seasoned workers into public service careers, including education.** The good news is that many people seeking greater meaning in their lives have considered making a move into education, health services, social services, local government, and various creative careers. Carol Peck, president and CEO of the Rodel Charitable Foundation, points out that "after experiencing the increased intensity, competition, and depersonalization of the job market, people are coming to place a higher value on loyalty and engagement in work environments—like teaching—that value relationships and the opportunity to change lives." She adds,

"Loyalty wears thin when money is the only source of fulfillment."

- **Paying more attention to emotional health.** For decades, educators have recognized the need to help people deal with their leisure time and pursue a broad range of interests, talents, and abilities. Schools and colleges play a key educational role in building an understanding of these skills. With limited life experience, students need skills to cope with situations that may seem overwhelming—a bad grade, the loss of a boyfriend or girlfriend, or being bullied. Gangs are identity groups, often providing a home base for people who feel they have been excluded or marginalized. A thoughtful array of essential life and leadership skills could help students find perspective and give them a framework for dealing with emotional trauma that might otherwise lead to self-destructive behavior. Emotional intelligence matters.

Understanding will grow that sustained poverty is expensive, debilitating, and unsettling.

Sustained Poverty ↔ Opportunity and Hope

In a fast-moving world, the distinction between haves and have-nots is broadening and becoming even clearer. Perhaps the most worrisome concern is the growth in "sustained poverty." We find it in our individual communities, in our nations, and worldwide. It's a situation that almost seems to be inherited. From generation to generation, it increases exponentially. For too many, hope is a long forgotten dream.

Poverty among children is not spread evenly. According to the U.S. Census Bureau, about 13 percent of White children younger than 18 live in poverty, compared with 27 percent of Hispanic and 30 percent of Black children.

That child who comes to school while being raised in poverty very likely does not benefit from the quality of health care and nutrition available to other children. Other disadvantages, right from the start, often include fewer learning resources at home, negative stereotyping, placement in lower tracks or ability groups, retention, an anti-school attitude and value system, and test bias, according to 2000 information from the U.S. Department of Education. In some cases, these children might have less qualified teachers in their classrooms, or their highly dedicated teachers might be frustrated by a lack of respect or parental involvement.[41]

"Why should we be concerned about sustained poverty?" "The poor will always be with us. What do we have to lose because some people are poor?" The answers are glaring: lost talent and productivity, human frustration, increased welfare and other subsidies; more gang activity, violence, and self-destructive behaviors; fuller jails; expansion of physical and mental health concerns; compromised performance in school; and a demonstrated lack of civility toward those in need. The anger that often accompanies poverty can lead to everything from crowded homeless shelters and soup kitchens to civil unrest, street protests, and terrorism, the unraveling of society.

The cost of sustained poverty is high. What more is at stake? Hope and human dignity.

Worldwide Concerns. Around the globe, people are often forced into poverty by natural disasters such as drought, authoritarian regimes, and a gross lack of educational or economic opportunity. Worldwide, immigrants often go through periods of poverty and sacrifice while they get a foothold on the ladder to accomplishment and reward. Consider also the estimated 13 million refugees who often have little more than the clothes on their backs, some living in camps for years on end.[42]

In 2004, the five countries with the highest gross domestic product per capita were: Luxemborg ($36,400), the United States ($36,200), Bermuda ($33,000), San Marino ($32,000), and Switzerland ($28,600), according to an aneki.com listing of the richest countries in the world. Those with the lowest GDP per capita, listed as the poorest countries in the world, were: Sierra Leone ($500), Tanzania ($550), Ethiopia ($560), Somalia ($600), and Cambodia ($710).[43]

What happens when vast numbers of young people, generally in their "coming of age" years of 16 to 24, are un- or under-educated and unemployed? We know from our own experience that many lose hope, become frustrated, and then get extremely angry. If they can garner the strength and support, they may take to the streets. If confronted with an opportunity to fight back, they might even turn to violence or terrorism to make their voices heard.

As the world population expands, poverty will multiply geometrically unless it is effectively addressed, within communities and nations and among nations. For many, crisis has already become catastrophe. The problems posed by sustained poverty will have profound implications for our individual and collective futures. Poverty is everyone's problem. In fact, poverty makes us all poor.

■ Implications for Education

- **Understanding the history and consequences of sustained poverty.** Schools and communities need a heightened understanding of the role poverty has played throughout history and the challenges it poses for the future. If we choose not to learn from history, then we may, indeed, be forced to relive it.

- **Offering education programs that prepare people to avoid or overcome poverty.** If students do not understand issues posed by poverty, they are probably not well educated. Rosa Smith, president of the Schott Foundation and a veteran superintendent, speculates, "Schools need to produce students capable of quickly mastering our ever-changing technology, with high levels of analysis and judgment skills." She also points out that, unless the problems posed by poverty are effectively addressed, students may have to realize that the future could hold less in resources for the middle class.

Betsy Rogers, the 2003 National Teacher of the Year, advocates "using incentives to recruit master teachers for our most needy schools, early intervention through preschool programs, and quality career tech programs at the high school level to help close the achievement gap between the affluent and the poverty stricken."

"The school must be the great equalizer while it is assuring high achievement for its students," Arnold Fege submits, noting that "this has never before been accomplished." He comments on the importance of "an investment in education, from birth to, in some cases, adulthood." Programs offered before and after school, tutoring, Head Start and other opportunities for early education, free and reduced-price lunches and other meals, counseling, and many other programs, at least in part, attempt to address challenges that accompany poverty.

Trend 15

*Pressure will grow for society to prepare people for jobs
and careers that may not currently exist.*

Career Preparation ↔ Career Adaptability

Turning out students who are employable—that's one of several
expectations we have for our education system, along with creating
good citizens who are relatively well adjusted, curious, persistent,
and ethical.

While career, vocational, and technical education, at all levels,
have always been important, they have very likely never been
facing such exponential change. "By 2015, more than half (some
argue 80 percent) of us will be working at jobs that don't exist
yet," says internationally respected forecaster Faith Popcorn,
founder of Faith Popcorn's BrainReserve, a future-oriented
marketing consultancy. Some predictions, she admits, "might
seem overly dramatic" but they "project the current rate of
change." Popcorn ventures, "Jobs that are commonplace today
will become museum pieces, along with buggy whip manufacturers, and typewriter repair people." Consider some new occupa-
tions that are coming on line:

- **Cybrarians.** These librarians of the Internet will try to get this
  fountain of information even better organized as it expands at
  more than a million pages a day.

- **Web Gardeners.** These busy people, much like cybrarians, will "keep web sites planted, weeded, inviting, and perfectly maintained," according to Popcorn. The Web gardeners and cybrarians might even attend the same cyber-convention.[44]

- **Robotic Engineers.** If you choose this occupation, expect to design, build, and maintain robots that transport people, go deep into mines, explore planets and satellites, probe the wreckage of destroyed buildings, defuse explosive devices, and even care for aging people or individuals with disabilities.[45]

- **Astrogeologists, Astrophysiologists, Astrobiologists.** People who hold these positions will study geology, people, and other organisms in space. On a longer journey, perhaps a trip of several years, expect a demand for astropsychologists.

- **Terrorism Analysts.** Many types of struggles, as we know, can trigger acts of terrorism. These analysts might be capable of studying everything from the sociological triggers for terrorism to the origins of materials used in the act.[46]

- **Automotive Fuel Cell Battery Technicians and Hybrid Technicians.** Someone will need to maintain these new cars, which are powered by a combination of gasoline or some other type of fuel and batteries. As hydrogen becomes more practical as a fuel of choice, we can expect more hydrogen fueling and electrical charging stations.[47]

- **Programming Artists.** These are people who develop virtual media and Hollywood animation, among other things. According to *Newsweek*, "The U.S. Labor Department projects employment for commercial artists to rise 25 percent by 2008, spurred by an increased demand for digital talent."[48]

• **A few more for consideration:** Fusion engineer, cryonics technician, tissue engineer, supply chain manager, and leisure consultant.

■ Implications for Education and Society

• **Schools and colleges will become centers for continuing education, training, and retraining.** "Schools will be natural centers for training for all ages, year-round, and for extended hours," predicts George Hollich, retired director of curriculum and summer programs for the Milton Hershey School in Pennsylvania. He speculates this trend may reveal an increased need for "day care, elder care, and neighborhood training programs." Many of these service providers "could be brought under one roof."

Michael Silver of Seattle University agrees. "Students will need to develop a disposition for continuous lifelong learning and take responsibility for their own career management," he says. To keep pace with changing employment needs, "students will need to reinvent themselves and redirect their skills," and they will need "to have the willingness and ability to respond quickly and flexibly to changing workforce needs."

• **Fresh approaches will be needed to teach career and entrepreneurial skills.** "Entrepreneurism can be taught as a simulation, using models that help students develop strategies to gauge economic demand, and then create and deliver products and services to meet changing circumstances," points out Carol Peck, president and CEO of the Rodel Charitable Foundation. "Every effort should be made to expose students to the many possibilities for career choices and the necessary flexibility it will take to adapt to changing economies and technologies."

"Attitude is also important," Peck remarks. "Curriculum and content should be designed to allow students opportunities to experience different roles and responsibilities as individuals in groups." Students will also need "practice assessing their own skills and creating positive profiles in the form of resumes and proposals for productive engagement in the economy," Peck suggests.

- **Education systems will need to understand changes in industries and careers, and be able and willing to adapt.** Emphasizing the importance of understanding history, Gary Rowe, president of Rowe, Inc., in Atlanta, Ga., points out "entire railroads disappeared, heavy industries turned to rust, and new technologies transformed workplaces." For high school students, "the expectation of change must be a part of their view of the world," he emphasizes.

"Seat time in the classroom is no guarantor of the skills needed for modern vocations and careers," Rowe adds. "The best way for students to absorb how to be entrepreneurial, how to manage, and how to be flexible comes with 'up out-of-the-seat' experiential learning." Those careers that capture the interest of students might turn out to be in either the for-profit or nonprofit sectors.

- **Communities will need to fully understand that their economic future may depend on their ability to understand rapid changes in technology and to maintain a workforce that will help them adapt in the future.** A community, or an industry for that matter, can no longer be content with simply doing one thing well and doing it forever. Those who thrive and survive will be the communities that encourage research and development, who support their educational institutions, and who pay particular attention to their mix of professionals'/workers' skills and attitudes. Whether they are competitive will also depend on the quality of life, the ethos or personality of their communities, and the ability to attract and keep knowledge workers.

Competition will increase to attract and keep qualified educators.

Demand →Higher Demand

The United States is faced with attracting around two million-plus teachers during the first decade of the 21st century. Not surprisingly, the U.S. Bureau of Labor Statistics (BLS) has said the demand for teachers will be "very high." Because of escalating enrollments and lower class sizes, BLS estimates that, by 2012, the actual numbers of elementary school teachers who will be needed will go up 15.2 percent, secondary school teachers up 18.2 percent, secondary vocational educators up 9.0 percent, preschool teachers up 36 percent, and postsecondary teachers up 38.1 percent.[49]

Looking globally, *cnn.com* reported in 2002 that "some 35 million more (teachers) are needed throughout the world" to be on track for meeting an "Education for All" goal set for 2015 by 83 countries.[50] Education is increasingly seen as the key factor in securing a brighter future. That's why leaders in a growing number of countries are busy trying to interest even more people in education careers.

As the nation and world move from an industrial age into a global knowledge/information age, demand is shifting from manufacturing to knowledge workers. That's what educators are, and that's why schools are facing more competition than ever for talented people. That competition is coming not just from the school district or college next door but from other public- and private-sector institutions.

In addition to teachers, school administrators will also be in high demand. Between 2002 and 2012, BLS predicts a 20.7 percent increase in the total number of administrators needed in elementary and secondary schools.[51] The American Association for Employment in Education (AAEE) points to a need for superintendents and principals, citing shortages at all levels—elementary, middle school, and high school. "As more of the individuals filling these positions reach retirement age, the shortage can be anticipated to increase," AAEE reported in 2000.[52]

■ Implications for Education

• **Providing the community with its number-one attraction.** What is the first question many people ask when considering where to live? "How are the schools?" Communities that invest in education and are determined to attract and keep the very best educators are making an investment not only in their children's future, but also in their future property values. They understand the interlocking connection between education and a community's economy, quality of life, and reputation.

• **Ensuring a qualified workforce.** Education is the key to developing a workforce that will attract business and industry and stimulate economic growth. Some communities have discovered that truth, and they are committed to building an infrastructure capable of producing creative, well-educated people. At the same time, they are recruiting knowledge workers who will then, in turn, insist on and support a 21st-century education for their children.

• **Setting up programs for recruiting and retaining outstanding educators.** For communities large and small, whether they are rural, suburban, or urban, recruitment and retention have become bottom-line issues in the quest to ensure "highly qualified" educators to prepare students for the future. Just putting an ad in the paper and waiting for people to break down the door may not work anymore. Competition is stiff, and that competition is coming from both inside and outside education.

- **Exercising caution in stretching the supply to meet the demand.** Gene Carter, executive director of the Association for Supervision and Curriculum Development (ASCD), has expressed concern about setting people up as teachers when they don't understand pedagogy. In a column titled, "Content Knowledge Without Pedagogy Shortchanges Students," he quotes a Hart/Teeter opinion poll commissioned by the Educational Testing Service. A majority of those responding said that "having skills to design learning experiences that inspire and interest children" is the most important attribute of a quality teacher.[53]

- **Assigning excellent teachers to schools where needs are greatest.** Complaints have been raised that go something like this, "You're assigning first-year teachers and teachers who are having problems somewhere else to schools where kids have the greatest needs and the parents are least demanding." In 2004, in fact, the U.S. Department of Education issued a complaint against a large urban school system stating that, "Qualified and skilled teachers—the most crucial 'input' in the district's instructional program—are inequitably distributed within the system, with more-qualified, more-experienced teachers going to the city's lower-minority, lower-poverty schools." In response, the district noted that it was strengthening its recruitment and professional development efforts and negotiating a new contract that could bring changes in the way teaching talent is distributed among schools.[54]

- **Improving preparation and professional development programs.** First, teachers and administrators need to be well prepared to ensure a sound education for their students. Second, unless they are well prepared for the realities they will face in teaching children or providing executive leadership for the institution, they may simply give up and do something else. Preparation programs at colleges and universities need constant upgrades to ensure they are equipping educators to get students ready for the future. Professional development programs should perhaps range from individual mentorships as a new teacher first sets foot in the classroom to ongoing knowledge, skill, and behavior-building activities.

- **Making teaching an international profession.** Many U.S. teachers currently work in international or military dependents schools around the world. According to the NEA, "As many as 10,000 foreign teachers work in the U.S. public school systems on 'nonimmigrant' or cultural exchange visits." In some cases, these temporary employees are "helping to address perceived teacher shortages, particularly in math, science, foreign languages, and special education, as well as in . . . poor urban and rural school districts." Increasingly, teaching will become an international profession, especially for those with a combination of subject matter expertise, a missionary spirit, an innate curiosity, and language skills.

- **Collaborating with the competition.** In the competition for talent, schools and colleges may not always win. The same businesses and other institutions that depend on the education system to turn out good citizens who are employable are generally quite comfortable hiring outstanding candidates who originally prepared to be teachers. In some cases, education systems may need to collaborate with the competition so that each can benefit from the talent that might otherwise be diverted from the classroom.

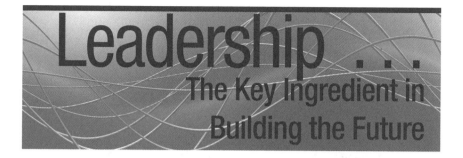

Leadership . . .
The Key Ingredient in Building the Future

As leaders in society, our responsibility is to constantly create the future we need, not just defend what we have.

Sixteen Trends . . . Their Profound Impact on Our Future is based on years of observations and research. Hundreds of academic and front-line sources contributed to the publication. However, the book is only the beginning. It can't stop there. It's not enough to simply read the book and let it gather dust on a shelf.

The next step depends on thoughtful, action-oriented, future-focused leadership. If schools and colleges, any institutions for that matter, hope to shape an even brighter future, they simply must consider the implications of these and other trends. For example, they need to ask, "What are the implications of these trends for how we operate the organization?" and "What are the implications of these trends for what students need to know and be able to do...their academic knowledge, skills, behaviors, and attitudes?"

In education, leadership is not confined to the front office. All educators should consider themselves leaders by virtue of the key roles they play in society. Our challenge is to not let the crush of important day-to-day issues, the meetings, email, and countless

Addressing the Sixteen Trends . . . Some Suggestions

As we noted in the introduction, this *Overview* is a condensation of *Sixteen Trends . . . Their Profound Impact on Our Future.* That publication, available from Educational Research Service (ERS) carries in-depth information about trends and their implications. It also suggests detailed approaches for using these trends in creating a strategic plan or living strategy, or possibly just breathing new life, energy, and enthusiasm into the organization. Here are a few steps we recommend:

- **First, obtain copies of** *Sixteen Trends . . . Their Profound Impact on Our Future* **(the publication on which this** *Overview* **is based) for as many people as possible, including those in leadership positions.** Consider using the *Overview* as a handout to stimulate thinking far and wide about forces affecting our institutions, including our communities. While the complete book is written to be of interest to the general reader, it has also been shaped to serve as a text for futures studies units and college/university courses.

- **Second, share this information with educators, parents, students, leaders in business and government, and others in the community.** Getting people to think about the future is an act of intellectual leadership. The books will help share information. So will presentations, news stories, seminars, conferences, and discussion groups. Ask people to pay serious attention to each trend and its implications. Have them think about action plans that include a commitment to staying in touch with issues and trends. Let everyone know that "staying in touch will help us become poised for the future."

- **Third, scan the environment.** Unless they constantly scan the environment, organizations, including schools and colleges, soon find themselves isolated and out of touch. How can we maintain a 24/7 connection with the world around us? One way is to systematically identify local, statewide/provincial, national, and international issues, and sort them according to their probability and possible impact. If an issue is high in probability and impact, we'd better pay attention to it and manage it. If we don't, it will manage us.

In addition to trends and issues analysis, we can scan the internal and external environment by using gap analysis, flexibility/innovation analysis, and PEST analysis, to name a few. PEST, by the way, stands for identifying the political, economic, social, and technological forces affecting our organization and society. Identifying the characteristics of the organization we want to become, coupled with scenario planning, can help us develop a vision for the future.

- **Fourth, formulate driving questions.** At the risk of repetition, here are a few: "What are the implications of these trends for how we run our school/college/business/foundation/government agency/nongovernmental organization/state/province/country?" "What are the implications of these trends for what students need to know and be able to do…their academic knowledge, skills, behaviors, and attitudes?" "What are the implications of these trends for economic growth and development and quality of life in our community?"

- **Fifth, convene Futures Councils.** Consider pulling together one or more Futures Councils. These groups, made up of both staff and community, should likely have rotating membership to involve greater numbers of people over time. Those involved represent the diversity of the community. Their purpose is not to grind axes or lobby for special interests but to thoughtfully study trends and issues and suggest possible implications for the institution. That thinking can be used as a resource as policies are considered and programs developed.

other stuff that keeps drifting into our lives stand in the way of creating a future. That commitment, after all, may be the essence of leadership.

Each day, we give hundreds of answers, but we have little time to think about whether we're asking the right questions. Things that worked two years ago may not be working now. Too often, we simply defend what we have, what's on top of our desks, rather than take the time to consider accelerating trends and their impact on our organizations and our communities.

How can we get a handle on the future? How can we demonstrate our own brand of intellectual leadership? How can we energize our education system and our community? How can we take needed steps that will lead us toward creating a new agenda for a new millennium?

We have a choice. We can sit back and take "whatever happens." Or, rather than limiting our response to the latest mandates, we can blaze our own trails. Using *Sixteen Trends . . . Their Profound Impact on Our Future* as a starting point, we can pave a better pathway, even a super highway, to the future. In the process, we'll generate the energy and commitment we so deeply need to ensure students get an excellent education and our organizations, communities, and nations thrive.

As leaders in society, our responsibility is to constantly create the future we need, not just defend what we have. The process of staying in touch with the environment, getting connected to the world of ideas and possibilities around us, staying on top of issues, and considering the implications of massive trends must be ongoing.

While we surely need to tackle today's problems, we simply can't take our eyes off the future. We have an opportunity to build an even better world, create what truly are learning organizations, demonstrate our ability to engage in knowledge creation and breakthrough thinking, and, in the process, build our own legacies.

Effective leaders understand the need to bring others on board. Leaders connect people and ideas. They bring them together in common purpose and build a sense of ownership. They tap the richness of thinking that is already there in schools, colleges, and other organizations, and in the community. When people are engaged, they're more likely to declare, "We're all in this together."

Sixteen Trends is not just a book. It is an opportunity!

The trends discussed in this book can present challenges for schools and other institutions. Depending on how we look at them, they also present substantial opportunities.

Archimedes said, "Give me a lever and a fulcrum and a place whereon to stand, and I'll move the world."[55] He was making a point that using the right levers and pulleys can make it possible for us to move objects that are greater than our own weights. *Sixteen Trends* provides us with not only a place to stand but also a lever and a fulcrum.

Our task, if we choose to accept it, is both complex and exciting. Let's use what we now know about trends to ensure our schools, colleges, communities, and nations are ready to prepare generations of students to live satisfying and productive lives in the 21st century.

References and Endnotes

[1] U.S. Census Bureau. (2004). *National population projections, summary files by age, sex, race, and Hispanic origin, 1998-2100.* (March 4, 2004). Washington, DC: Author. Retrieved from http://census.gov/population

[2] National Center for Health Statistics. (n.d.). *Life expectancy* (Data for the U.S. in 2001). Washington, DC: Author. Retrieved November 17, 2003, from http://www.cdc.gov/nchs/fastats/lifeexpect.htm

[3] Administration on Aging, U.S. Department of Health and Human Services. (1999). A profile of older Americans 1999. *AARP Report.* Washington, DC: American Association of Retired Persons, 1.

[4] Wallace, P. (1999). *Agequake: Riding the demographic rollercoaster shaking business, finance, and our world.* London: Nicholas Brealey, 6.

[5] U.S. Census Bureau. (2002). *National population projections, summary profiles, total population by age, sex, race, and Hispanic origin, middle series, 1999-2100.* (August 2, 2002). Washington, DC: Author.

[6] U.S. Census Bureau. (2003). Table 1. No. HS 13. Live births, deaths, infant deaths, and maternal deaths, 1900-2001. *Statistical abstract of the U.S. 2003.* Washington, D.C.: Author. Retrieved March 3, 2004, from http://census.gov/statab/hist/HS-13.pdf

[7] National Center for Health Statistics, U.S. Department of Health and Human Services. (2004). Births and deaths in the U.S. In *World almanac, book of facts, 2004* (p. 73). New York: World Almanac Education Group.

[8] *Ibid.*

[9] *Ibid,* and Ventura, S., Martin, J., Curtin, S.; Matthews, T.J, & Park, M. (2000). Table 1, Births: Final data for 1998. *National Vital Statistics Reports, 48*(3). In Marx, G. (2000). *Ten trends . . . Educating children for a profoundly different future* (p. 1). Arlington, VA: Educational Research Service.

[10] U.S. Census Bureau. (2004). *Sources of population growth.* Retrieved March 4, 2004, from http://www.npg.org/popfacts.htm

[11] U.S. Census Bureau. (1999). World population profile: 1998—Highlights (p. 2). (Updated version, March 18, 1999). Retrieved March 3, 2004, from http://www.census.gov/ipc/www/wp98001.html.

[12] National Center for Education Statistics. (2004). *Projections of education statistics to 2012,* Table 1-Enrollment in grades K-8 and 9-12 of elementary and secondary schools, by control of institution, from fall 1987 to fall 2012. Retrieved March 5, 2004, from http://www.nces.gov/pubs2002/proj2012/table_01.asp

[13] Yasin, S. (1999). The supply and demand of elementary and secondary school teachers in the United States. *ERIC Digest* (ED436529). (December 1999). Washington, DC: ERIC Clearinghouse on Teaching and Teacher Education, 1.

[14] U.S. Census Bureau. (2002). *National population profiles, total population by age, sex, race, and Hispanic origin.* (Rev. ed.). Retrieved August 2, 2002, from http://www.census.gov/population/www/projections/natsum-T3.html

[15] U.S. Census Bureau. (2000). *Projections of the resident population by age, sex, race, and Hispanic origin: 1999-2100, NP-D1-A.* Retrieved January 13, 2000, from http://www.census.gov

[16] U.S. Census Bureau. (2004). Sources of population growth. Retrieved March 9, 2004, from http://www.npg.org/popfacts.htm

[17] U.S. Census Bureau. (2000). *Components of change for the total resident population, middle series, 1999-2100 (natural increase, births, deaths, net migration, net change).* (January 13, 2000). Retrieved May 4, 2004, from http://www.census.gov/population/projections/nation/summary/np-t6-a.txt

[18] Ventura, M.C., et al. (2000). 24 (Table 1) and 30 (Table 6). In Marx, G., *Ten trends . . . Educating children for a profoundly different future* (p. 14). Arlington, VA: Educational Research Service.

[19] Kotkin, J. (1992). *Traces . . . How race, religion, and identity determine success in the new global economy.* New York: Random House, 3-4, 255.

[20] Marx, G. (2000). *Ten trends . . . Educating children for a profoundly different future.* Arlington, VA: Educational Research Service, 19.

[21] Perelman, L. (1997). Leading lights, an interview with Tom Stewart. *Knowledge Inc.* Retrieved March 10, 2004, from http://www.webcom.com/quantera/llistewart.html

[22] Bennis, W. (2002.). Becoming a leader of leaders. In Gibson, R., & Bennis, W. (2002). *Rethinking the future.* (p. 149). London: Nicholas Brealey.

[23] Robert Putnam, addressing a White House conference on the new economy. (April 5, 2000, Washington, DC).

[24] Richey, K.W. (1997). *The ENIAC.* Retrieved February 16, 1997, from the Virginia Tech Web site, http://www.ei.cs.vt.edu

[25] Cetron, M., & Cetron, K. (unpublished). *Education is the future.* Paper prepared in 2004 as members of the *Creating a Future* Advisory Council (Falls Church, VA).

[26] Breslau, K., & Chung, J. (2002). Big future in tiny spaces . . . Nanotechnology is moving from labs to businesses. *Newsweek* (Special Report, September 23, 2002), 48.

[27] Strauss, W., & Howe, N. (1991). *Generations: The history of America's future, 1584-2069.* New York: William Morrow, 36.

[28] Withrow, F., Long, H., & Marx, G. (1999). *Preparing schools and school systems for the 21st century.* Arlington, VA: American Association of School Administrators, 9.

[29] Gelb, M.J. (1998). *How to think like Leonardo da Vinci.* New York: Dell (Random House), 17.

[30] Marx, 62.

[31] Florida, R. (2002). *The rise of the creative class.* Cambridge, MA: Basic Books (Perseus Books Group), 33.

[32] Wilson, E.O. (1998). *Consilience . . . The unity of knowledge.* New York: Borzoi (Alfred A. Knopf), 113.

[33] Daggett, W.R. (1996). The challenge to America's schools: Preparing students for the 21st century. *School Business Affairs*. (April 1996), 10.

[34] Gibson, R. (2002). Rethinking the future. *Rethinking business*. London: Nicholas Brealey, 10-11.

[35] Withrow, F., Long, H., & Marx, G. (1999). *Preparing schools and school systems for the 21st century*. Arlington, VA: American Association of School Administrators, 14.

[36] James Wolfensohn, former president of the World Bank, addressing a White House conference on the new economy. (April 5, 2000, Washington, DC).

[37] Vedantam, S. (2005). Report on global ecosystems calls for radical changes. *The Washington Post*. (March 30, 2005), A2.

[38] Cover headlines, *Fortune* (July 16, 2001), and *Kiplinger's Personal Finance* (August 2001).

[39] Davis, K., & Franklin, M.B. (2001). Simplify. *Kiplinger's Personal Finance*. (August 2001), 66.

[40] Gardner, G. (2002). *Invoking the spirit*. Washington, DC: The Worldwatch Institute, 11.

[41] Ansell, S. (2004). Achievement gap. *Education Week* Issue Paper. March 18, 2004. Retrieved May 6, 2004, from http://www.edweek.org

[42] U.S. Committee for Refugees. (2003). The world's refugees, 2002. World refugee survey, 2003. In *World almanac and book of facts, 2004*. New York: World Almanac Education Group, 857.

[43] Aneki.com. (2004). *Richest countries in the world*. Retrieved March 3, 2004, from http://www.aneki.com/richest.html; and, *Poorest countries in the world*. Retrieved same date from http://www.aneki.com/poorest.html

[44] Popcorn, F., & Hanft, A. (2001). *Dictionary of the future*. New York: Hyperion, 300, 307.

[45] Breslau, K., & Chung, J. (2002). Big future in tiny spaces. *Newsweek*. (September 23, 2002), 56.

[46] Popcorn & Hanft, 306.

[47] Cetron, M. (2001). Forecasts for the next 25 years. *Forecasting international*. Bethesda, MD: World Future Society.

[48] Breslau, K, & Chung, J. (2002). Big future in tiny spaces. *Newsweek*. (September 23, 2002), 56.

[49] U.S. Department of Labor. (2004). *Occupation report, average annual job openings, 2002-2012*. Retrieved March 30, 2004, from http://www.bls.gov

[50] Cable News Network (CNN). (Online). (2002). *U.N.: Global education gulf deepening*. Retrieved November 14, 2002, from http://www.cnn.com

[51] U.S. Department of Labor, Bureau of Labor Statistics. (2004). *Occupation report, average annual job openings, 2002-2012, education administrators, elementary and secondary schools*. Retrieved March 30, 2004, from http://www.bls.gov

[52] American Association for Employment in Education. (2001). *Educator supply and demand in the United States, 2000 research report*. Columbus, OH: Author, 7.

[53] Carter, G.R. (2002). Content knowledge without pedagogy shortchanges students. *Is it good for the kids?* (Issue paper, August 2002). Alexandria, VA: Association for Supervision and Curriculum Development.

[54] Hendrie, C. (2004). Philadelphia teacher assignments questioned in complaint. *Education Week*. (March 17, 2004), 4.

[55] See: *Hutchinson Encyclopedia of Science*. "Archimedes." (Helicon Publishing, Oxford, U.K., 1998, p. 49), and *World Book Encyclopedia*, "Archimedes," (Field Enterprises Educational Corp., Chicago, IL, 1971, Vol. A, pp. 564-565).

Creating a Future Council of Advisors

Members of the Creating a Future Council of Advisors responded to either one or two rounds of questionnaires. In the first, advisors were asked to identify significant trends and issues that might affect education and society in the early part of the 21st century. In the second, they were asked to share what they considered the implications of a cluster of three trends and to comment on the importance of leaders capable of making connections in a complex, fast-moving world.

The Council's views helped shape the book, *Sixteen Trends . . . Their Profound Impact on Our Future*, published by Educational Research Service, as well as *Future-Focused Leadership: Preparing Schools, Students, and Communities for Tomorrow's Realities*, published by the Association for Supervision and Curriculum Development. Views expressed in these publications do not necessarily reflect the beliefs or opinions of any member of the Council or the Council as a whole, nor do they reflect the official views of ERS.

Drew Allbritten, executive director, Council for Exceptional Children, Arlington, Va.

Kenneth Bird, superintendent, The Westside Community Schools, Omaha, Neb.

Ted Blaesing, superintendent, White Bear Lake Area Schools, White Bear Lake, Minn.

Carol Brown, 2003-04 president, National School Boards Association, Alexandria, Va.

Kimberley Cetron, teacher, Fairfax County, Va., Public Schools

Marvin Cetron, president, Forecasting International, Ltd., Falls Church, Va.

Joseph F. Coates, president, Consulting Futurist, Inc., Washington, D.C.

Kenneth Dragseth, superintendent of schools, Edina, Minn., and 2003 National Superintendent of the Year

Marc Ecker, 2003-04 president, National Middle School Association, and superintendent of the Fountain Valley, Calif., schools

Arnold Fege, president, Public Advocacy for Kids, Annandale, Va.

Douglas Greenberg, president and CEO, Survivors of the Shoah Visual History Foundation, Los Angeles, Calif.

Elizabeth L. Hale, president, Institute for Educational Leadership, Washington, D.C.

Jane Hammond, superintendent in residence, Stupski Foundation, Mill Valley, Calif.

Linda Hodge, 2003-05 president, National PTA, Chicago, Ill.

George Hollich, (retired) director of curriculum and summer programs, Milton Hershey School, Hershey, Pa.

David Hornbeck, president of the Children's Defense Fund; former president and CEO, International Youth Foundation, Baltimore, Md.

John Hoyle, professor of educational administration, Texas A&M University, College Station, Tx.

Ryan Hunter, junior high school student, Long Island, N.Y.

Rick Kaufman, executive director, public engagement and communication, Jefferson County Public Schools, Colo., and 2003-04 president, National School Public Relations Association

Keith Marty, superintendent, School District of Menomonee Falls, Wisc.

Radwan Masmoudi, founder and president, Center for the Study of Islam and Democracy, Washington, D.C.

Frank Method, director, education policy, Research Triangle Institute, International, Washington, D.C.

Graham T.T. Molitor, president, Public Policy Forecasting, Potomac, Md., and vice president and legal counsel, World Future Society, Bethesda, Md.

Bob Mooneyham, executive director, National Rural Education Association, Norman, Okla.

Carol G. Peck, president and CEO, Rodel Charitable Foundation, Scottsdale, Ariz.

James Rickabaugh, superintendent, Whitefish Bay Schools, Whitefish Bay, Wisc.

Betsy Rogers, teacher, Jefferson County School System, Birmingham, Ala., and 2003 National Teacher of the Year

Gary Rowe, president, Rowe Inc., Lawrenceville, Ga.

Douglas Shiok, superintendent, Orange North Supervisory Union (school district), Williamstown, Vt.

Michael Silver, assistant professor of educational administration at Seattle University and a veteran superintendent

Rosa Smith, president, Schott Foundation for Public Education, Cambridge, Mass.

Ted Stilwill, former director, Iowa Department of Education, Des Moines, Iowa, and 2004 president, Council of Chief State School Officers, Washington, D.C.

David Pearce Snyder, consulting futurist, The Snyder Family Enterprise, Bethesda, Md.

V. Wayne Young, executive director, Kentucky Association of School Administrators, Frankfort, Ky.

ORDER FORM

Quantity	Title and Item Number	Base Price	ERS Individual Subscriber Price	ERS School District Subscriber Price	Total Price
	An Overview of Sixteen Trends... Their Profound Impact on Our Future (#0633)	$14	$10.50	$7	
	Sixteen Trends... Their Profound Impact on Our Future (#0630)	$30	$22.50	$15	

** Please double for international orders.

Shipping and Handling ** (Add the greater of $4.50 or 10% of purchase price.):	
Express Delivery ** (Add $20 for second-business-day service.):	
TOTAL DUE:	

SATISFACTION GUARANTEED!
If you are not satisfied with an ERS resource, return it in its original condition within 30 days of receipt, and we will give you a full refund.

Method of payment:

☐ Check enclosed (payable to Educational Research Service).

☐ Purchase order enclosed (P.O.#_____).

Bill my: ☐ VISA ☐ MasterCard ☐ American Express

Name on Card (print) _____

Account Number _____   Expiration Date _____

Signature _____   Date _____

Visit us online at www.ers.org for a complete listing of resources!

Shipping address:

☐ Dr. ☐ Mr. ☐ Mrs. ☐ Ms.   Name _____

Position _____   ERS Subscriber ID# _____

School District or Agency _____

Street Address _____

City _____   State _____   Zip _____

Phone _____   Fax _____   Email _____

Return completed order form to: Educational Research Service
1001 North Fairfax Street, Suite 500, Alexandria, VA 22314
Phone: 800-791-9308 • Fax: 800-791-9309 • Email: ers@ers.org • Web site: www.ers.org